Cool Stuff About Earth

Pauline Cartwright

Contents

Earth

Hi! I'm Zudu, your tour guide for Earth. We're about to enter Earth's **solar system.** So are you ready for a quick spin around Earth? Just don't let the humans see you!

Earth is the third planet from the Sun. Earth is the only planet that humans know about which has **liquid** water on it.

Earth's solar system includes the Sun and everything that travels around it.

Earth's Gravity

What is gravity?

Gravity surrounds Earth. It is a strong **force** pulling all objects towards the middle of Earth. Without gravity, everything would float away from Earth!

Gravity keeps all people on Earth!

Earth's moon also has gravity but its gravity is not as strong as Earth's gravity. That's why astronauts on the Moon moved with big, floaty steps!

Water on Earth

How much water is on Earth?

There is a *huge* amount of water on Earth. Water covers over 70% of the Earth's surface.

The oceans make up most of Earth's water. Water is also found in rivers, lakes, and in ice.

The longest river on Earth is the River Nile, in Africa.

If all the ice in the world melted, the seas would rise by about 70 metres. Many places on Earth would be flooded.

Why is the sea salty?

Much of the salt in the sea comes from rocks on the land. River water runs over rocks that **contain** salts. So the river water becomes slightly salty. The river then flows into the ocean. The ocean becomes more and more salty!

There is a salt lake on Earth called The Dead Sea. It is the saltiest body of water on Earth. This is because the rocks on the mountains around it are salty. The Dead Sea has so much salt in it that you can float without even trying!

Where do humans find water to drink?

Most of the water on Earth is salt water. But humans on Earth cannot drink this water. They need to drink water that is not salty. This water can be found in lakes, rivers and streams. It can also be frozen or can be found under the ground.

The fresh water found in lakes, streams and rivers has a small amount of salt in it, but people can still drink it.

People make dams and lakes to catch rain water or river water.

Dry Places on Earth

Where is the driest place on Earth?

Put on your snow clothes because we are off to Antarctica. Almost all of Antarctica is covered with ice. But it is the driest place on Earth!

Antarctica's Dry Valleys have had no rainfall for over 2 million years! It's very cold in the Dry Valleys. No living things can **survive** there.

Parts of the Dry Valleys have lakes under the snow and ice, but no rainfall.

A warm desert with no rain

The Atacama Desert in South America is also very, very dry. This desert gets very little rain. Some parts of the Atacama Desert have had no rain for 400 years. Some parts in the desert have never had rain!

Even though the Atacama Desert is very dry, some animals still live there. These include birds, lizards and mice.

Sand

Where does sand come from?

Sand grains are very hard. This is because these sand grains were once rock. Rocks are broken up and turned into sand by the wind and water. This takes many, many, many millions of years to happen!

Water can slowly break down rock over time.

Low hills of sand are called dunes. Wind can move sand dunes.

The Sky

Why is the sky blue?

Light from the Sun is made up of all the colours of the rainbow. Most of the Sun's light passes straight through Earth's **atmosphere**, apart from blue light. Blue light is scattered around the sky. So when you look at the sky, you see all this blue light!

When can you see rainbows?

The colours of the rainbow are red, orange, yellow, green, blue, indigo and violet. To remember their order, think of this name: ROY G BIV. You can only see rainbows when it is raining and when the Sun is low in the sky, and when its light shines through the raindrops.

Why are sunsets and sunrises red?

When the Sun rises and sets, the sky is a red, orange or pink colour.

At sunset or sunrise, the Sun is lower in the sky, so its light must travel further to get to Earth. Also, it must travel through more of Earth's atmosphere. This means more of the light is scattered and the Sun looks less bright. This also means that most of the blue light is so scattered now, it doesn't even reach the Earth. So, you see the red and orange colours!

Thunder and Lightning

What causes thunder and lightning?

What's that? It's a thunder storm. Can you hear the thunder and see the lightning?

Thunderstorms happen a lot in spring and summer.

Thunder storms happen when there is a lot of warm air near the ground. As this air rises, it becomes cooler and turns into heavy, dark clouds, full of ice and raindrops. The rumbling sound of thunder is when the warm air meets the cooler air.

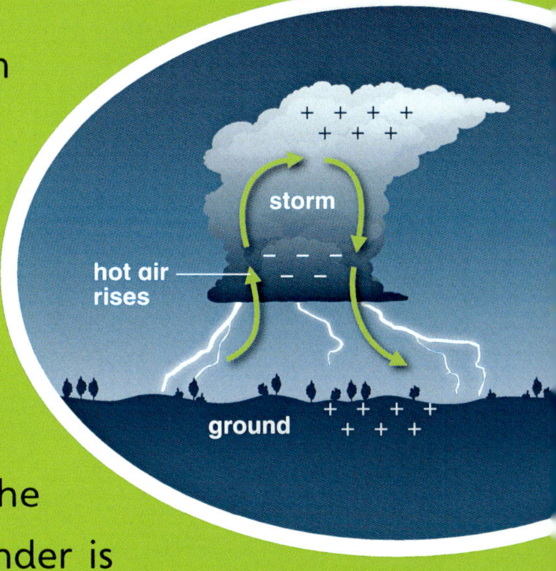

When there is thunder, there is lightning. Lightning is an electric, hot spark. Lightning happens when lots of small bits of ice in a storm cloud bump into each other. There is a lot of electricity in the storm clouds.

Lightning does not often hit the ground but when it does, it can strike trees and buildings, and cause fires.

The Wind

What makes the wind?

Wind is made because the Sun warms Earth's air. Warm air goes up. As warm air goes up, a rush of cold air moves in under it. This makes wind.

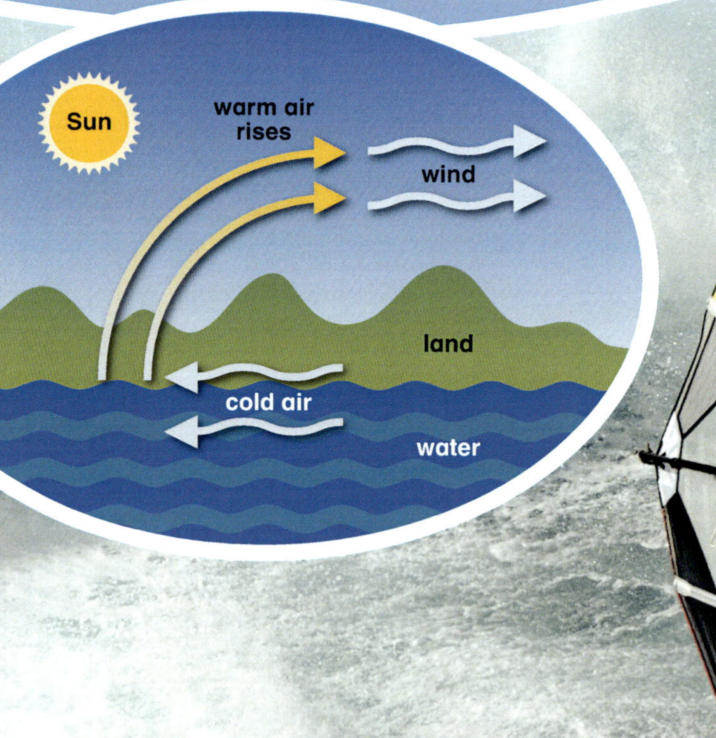

Wind moves over land and sea. The wind that moves over the land is often warmer than the wind over the sea. So most of Earth's coldest winds come in from the sea!

Remember: warm air goes up! That's what makes hot air balloons move upwards.

Earthquakes and Volcanoes

What makes an earthquake?

Earth is made up of rocks and liquid. The top part of Earth is made of huge plates of rock. Just under these plates is melting, **oozing** rock. The huge plates move slightly on top of the melting rocks.

The collapsed Cypress Freeway in Oakland, USA, after the 1989 Loma Prieta earthquake.

When the edges of plates push past each other, they shake and rumble. This is an earthquake.

What makes a volcano erupt?

We know about Earth's huge plates and melting rocks. But below them, there are rocks that have melted into very hot liquid. This liquid rock is called magma.

Sometimes, the magma bursts up through the earth, in between the huge plates. This is a volcano erupting!

Earth Quiz

So that's the end of our tour of Earth! We'll come back another time. There is still so much to learn!

Now, what did **you** learn about Earth? Try this quiz!

1. Why can't you drink most of Earth's water?
2. What is the force that stops you floating off into space?
3. What sound can be heard when warm air meets cool air?
4. What is the name of liquid rock under the ground?

Answers

1 Because most of Earth's water is salt water
2 Gravity **3** Thunder **4** Magma

Glossary

atmosphere	the gases surrounding Earth
contain	to have as a part of something
force	a power, a strength
liquid	a kind of fluid, such as water
oozing	slowly moving, squeezing through
solar system	the Sun and everything in space that travels around it
survive	to remain alive